THE NEOLITHIC REVOLUTION

THE FIRST HUMANS AND
EARLY CIVILIZATIONS

THE NEOLITHIC REVOLUTION

Susan Meyer

ROSEN
PUBLISHING®
New York

Published in 2017 by The Rosen Publishing Group, Inc.
29 East 21st Street, New York, NY 10010

First Edition

Library of Congress Cataloging-in-Publication Data

Names: Meyer, Susan, author.
Title: The neolithic revolution / Susan Meyer.
Description: New York : Rosen Publishing, 2017. | Series: The first humans
 and early civilizations | Includes bibliographical references and index.
Identifiers: LCCN 2015049237 | ISBN 9781499463248 (library bound) | ISBN
 9781499463224 (pbk.) | ISBN 9781499463231 (6-pack)
Subjects: LCSH: Neolithic period—Juvenile literature.
Classification: LCC GN775 .M47 2016 | DDC 930.1/4—dc23
LC record available at http://lccn.loc.gov/2015049237

Manufactured in China

CONTENTS

INTRODUCTION...6

CHAPTER 1
A WORLD CHANGES...9

CHAPTER 2
CHANGE FROM THE GROUND UP...20

CHAPTER 3
TAMING THE WILD BEASTS...27

CHAPTER 4
WHAT LED TO THE NEOLITHIC REVOLUTION?...35

CHAPTER 5
HUMANITY AFTER THE NEOLITHIC REVOLUTION...40

TIMELINE...51

GLOSSARY...53

FOR MORE INFORMATION...55

FOR FURTHER READING...58

BIBLIOGRAPHY...60

INDEX...62

INTRODUCTION

Life today is full of things we take for granted. For example, it's assumed that modern people live together in organized societies. You likely live in a neighborhood or even in a bustling city. Even people who live in rural areas are connected to many other people. We have governments to build roads, post offices, and schools for everyone to use. And these days, you probably don't grow most of the food you eat. Instead you get your vegetables, meats, and grains from a grocery store or supermarket. Food is grown or raised on big commercial farms and shipped around the country. Life wasn't always the way it is today. Around twelve thousand years ago, humans didn't have any of these aspects that today seem to us to be a critical part of humanity.

Humans evolved to *Homo sapiens*, the species we are today, around two hundred thousand years ago. The first humans lived in Africa, and around one hundred thousand years ago, they spread to other parts of the world. The continents of Asia and North America were connected by ice back then, so people were able to travel far and wide. They had many reasons to be on the move. They needed to follow animals that they could hunt for food. They also caught fish and gathered berries, wild vegetables, and grains for food. If they stayed in one place for too long or an area became too populated, there wouldn't be enough resources for everyone to survive.

The Knap of Howar in Scotland is one of the oldest surviving human settlements in northern Europe. These stone houses were occupied between 3600 and 2700 BCE.

Then around 10,000 to 8000 BCE, everything changed. People learned to grow their own food. They also domesticated animals that could be raised for food or kept to help work the fields. The beginning of agriculture and the domestication of animals were two of the biggest developments in human history. This remarkable period is called the Neolithic Revolution, or sometimes the agricultural revolution. A revolution is a dramatic and far-reaching change.

Thanks to the advances made during the Neolithic Revolution, people could produce food much more efficiently. This meant that the same area of land could provide food for a larger population. People could also control the amount of food around them without having to move all of the time. Both of these factors contributed to people being able to settle in one place and stop being nomadic. With more people living together, groups of people began to make up rules and create organized societies and hierarchies. Now that people were not moving around all the time, they were able to create new crafts and architecture. Some people became specialists in farming and raising animals for food, while others focused on these new pursuits. This created a need for economy and trade. Governments developed, as larger groups of people living together needed more laws and leadership.

The Neolithic Revolution didn't happen all at once everywhere. As explained above, people were spread out all across the world at this time. Some places where the climate was better for agriculture, like an area called the Fertile Crescent in the Middle East, experienced the Neolithic Revolution sooner than other places. The Neolithic Revolution occurred during the Neolithic period, also known as the New Stone Age. The Neolithic period started around 10,000 BCE. It followed the Paleolithic and Mesolithic periods, in which people used simple tools. It came before the Bronze Age, during which people—using all the advances they developed from the Neolithic period—began using metal tools.

The importance of the Neolithic Revolution and the changes that occurred in the ways humans lived during that time cannot be overstated. So much of what we take for granted as part of modern humanity has its roots firmly planted in the beginnings of agriculture.

CHAPTER 1
A WORLD CHANGES

Before considering all the ways the Neolithic Revolution turned the world upside down, it is important to look at what humans were doing prior to it. The Paleolithic period, also known as the Old Stone Age, lasted for the majority of human history. It started about 3.3 million years ago and ended about 12,000 years ago—or around 10,000 BCE. If you consider the fact that humans have been around for millions of years, the period of time in which we developed all of our culture and technology is actually a tiny fraction of a percent of our time on Earth. During the Paleolithic period, people were living as hunters and gatherers, fishing and following game all across the planet in search of food. Over time, Paleolithic people developed crude stone tools by chipping away at soft rocks to form arrowheads and knives.

Before reaching the Neolithic period, humans in some parts of the world experienced what archaeologists call the Mesolithic period, or Middle Stone Age. At this time, humans were still hunting and gathering and living a nomadic lifestyle. Much like today's people, humans who lived in the past were very good at creating technology to help make their lives easier. During the Mesolithic period, they made advances in tools that made their hunting more efficient. They created better stone tools, which helped them to hunt and fish a wider variety of animals. They created tools specialized to their environments and the animals and plants that lived there. The Mesolithic period occurred at different times in different parts of the globe. During both the Paleolithic period and the Mesolithic period, people spent a lot of their energy on finding enough food to stay alive. They didn't have time to do much else. While some art exists from this time—cave painting and stone carvings, for example—most of the artifacts are useful tools.

Humanity's real show started when the Neolithic Revolution began. As people around the world discovered that they could plant seeds to grow grains, vegetables, and fruits, they had more of a reason to stay put in one place because they wanted to collect the harvest. As a result, permanent settlements were established. Neolithic people also began domesticating plants and animals. At first the plants they planted and animals they cared for were basically wild. Over time, though, these species gradually took on the characteristics of the domesticated plants and animals we know today.

CENTERS OF CHANGE

Today, the world is so connected by the Internet and other media that changes are heard around the globe very quickly. In the Neolithic period, things operated a little differently. The results of the Neolithic Revolution slowly spread globally, over a period of thousands of

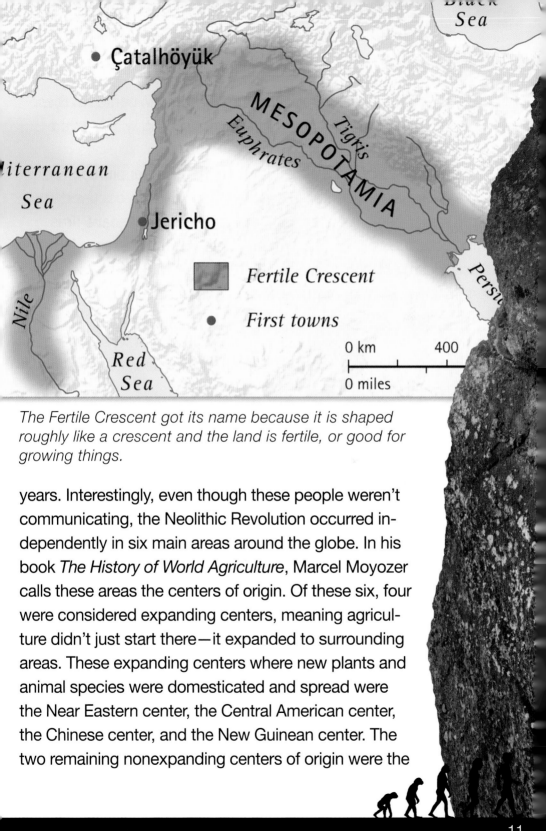

The Fertile Crescent got its name because it is shaped roughly like a crescent and the land is fertile, or good for growing things.

years. Interestingly, even though these people weren't communicating, the Neolithic Revolution occurred independently in six main areas around the globe. In his book *The History of World Agriculture*, Marcel Moyozer calls these areas the centers of origin. Of these six, four were considered expanding centers, meaning agriculture didn't just start there—it expanded to surrounding areas. These expanding centers where new plants and animal species were domesticated and spread were the Near Eastern center, the Central American center, the Chinese center, and the New Guinean center. The two remaining nonexpanding centers of origin were the

South American center and the North American center. In these places, agriculture appeared but did not spread widely to the surrounding areas.

The first and perhaps best known of the centers of origin is the Near Eastern center. The Neolithic Revolution occurred in the Near East in the area known as the Fertile Crescent. This includes the northern part of the Nile River, the eastern Mediterranean, and the area around the Tigris and Euphrates Rivers in what is now Iraq. As the name suggests, this area was full of fertile land perfect for growing crops. There were pistachio trees, wild grains (such as barley), and early types of wheat (such as spelt and emmer wheat). Rabbit, boars, deer, gazelles, and other wild animals were also plentiful.

In the Chinese center, the first Neolithic farmers became the Yangshao civilization along the Yellow River. It is no surprise that all of the centers of origin occurred along major rivers. Plentiful freshwater was critical for a civilization to arise and stay in one place. Rivers provided not only water but also silt, which makes the ground around them fertile. Silt is a mineral-rich, sand-like substance carried by rivers. It is left on the ground as a river changes course over time and makes the land better for growing plants. Along the Yellow River, the Neolithic Revolution began around 10,000 BCE. There is evidence that people in this area grew cabbage and turnips. They also raised mulberry trees to feed silkworms. There is also evidence that they raised oxen and pigs.

Sewing the First Seeds at Jericho

One of the earliest Neolithic settlements was Jericho, in the Jordan River Valley. Today, Jericho is a city in the West Bank. Thirteen thousand years earlier, nomadic hunters and gatherers came to this valley. They found it full of trees and freshwater lakes. Gazelles and wild cattle roamed the land. There were so many resources to rely on that the people simply decided to stay. They had no reason to keep moving because everything they needed was there.

The people built stone houses with roofs made of wood from the surrounding trees. They gathered grain and stored it in baskets during the winter. They began to develop a culture. They wore jewelry and carved figurines from stone. These people were called the Natufian.

It is not clear if the Natufian ever farmed the land, but that development would come to Jericho soon. Around eleven thousand years ago, the people in Jericho began throwing seed onto the fertile ground and discovered that it sprouted! They could now harness the power of producing their own food.

The Chinese center expanded east to the valley of the Yangtze River and new cultures developed there. These cultures began planting rice, domesticating the grain from wild grasses that grew there naturally. In this area, there is evidence of people collecting wild rice to eat dating to 10,000 to 9000 BCE. Evidence of domesticated rice, more similar to what we eat today, dates to around 8000 to 6000 BCE. Rice grew very well in the moist soil along the river. Growing rice quickly

This vessel, called a ping, was used to carry water by the Neolithic Yangshao people who lived along the Yellow River.

spread to other parts of what is now China, as well as to other places in eastern Asia. Between 3000 and 2000 BCE, rice growing spread to Southeast Asia and from there to the Indian subcontinent.

In the Central American center, sometimes known as Mesoamerica, the first agriculture began in the south of Mexico. Proof of the Neolithic Revolution ranges there from 7000 to 2000 BCE. Nomadic

Maize, or corn, was one of the foundational crops of Central American agriculture. Today, maize is a staple crop for many people around the world.

hunters and gatherers began raising peppers and avocados. At first these early farmers grew vegetables seasonally. They formed temporary villages, gathered wild vegetables, and hunted animals for meat. Soon they graduated to raising other vegetables, including maize (corn), squash, and pumpkin. They also domesticated animals like bees and turkeys. The process was slow. At first, people supplemented the food that they gathered with food that they grew. In time, they settled down and survived primarily off of agriculture. This process began in about 7000 BCE and continued over the next several thousand years. Over this time, these people became dependent on what is known as the Mesoamerican Triad: maize, beans, and squash. These three foods became staples of their diets.

The New Guinea center refers to the activities on an island in the South Pacific: Papua New Guinea. The island is north of Australia and west of Indonesia. Some scientists believe that people here began growing taro (a type of root vegetable) around twenty-eight thousand years

New Guinea is an island located in the southwestern Pacific Ocean, north of the continent of Australia. It is the world's second largest island.

ago—before the Neolithic Revolution really began in most places. This would make Papua New Guinea home to some of the first farmers in the world. It is hard to determine exactly when intentional taro growing began through archaeological evidence because little evidence remains. Scientists think that, at first, the farmers of New Guinea grew taro plants in the forest. By about 7000 BCE, they had figured out how to enclose land and grow plants in separate gardens. They built walls to keep wild pigs, and later domesticated pigs, from eating what they'd planted.

TECHNOLOGY ON THE MOVE

So how did knowledge spread throughout the world from these four centers? It was a gradual process taking place over thousands of years. While people stopped living a nomadic existence, it didn't mean they didn't ever move and spread out. As their populations grew, they would expand to nearby lands. If those lands were occupied, they would colonize nearby groups of hunters and gatherers. Tools and ideas that made life easier were easy to convince others to try. Initially, people spread out along rivers because that was the easiest place to farm. Over time, they ventured out away from rivers and into plains and forests. There they discovered ways to turn these environments into farmland, too. Depending on the plants they were farming, they would sometimes plant them among the trees. If they needed the full space, they would burn down the trees in a method called slash-and-burn farming. To make the plains easier to farm, people would divert water from rivers to create basic irrigation systems.

From the Near Eastern center, people spread northward into Europe along the Danube River.

Archaeologists have found tools in the early settlements there that are of Near Eastern origin. Near Eastern farming technology also spread south into what would become Egypt along the Nile River and then further into Africa. As mentioned above, rice growing spread from the Chinese center across much of Southeast Asian and beyond. Maize production in the Central American center spread both north and south

Archaeologists have uncovered evidence of irrigation channels created by Neolithic peoples to bring water to their crops.

into both North and South America. The growing of taro in Papua New Guinea spread to surrounding islands—west to Indonesia and east to the Solomon Islands.

North and South America were home to the two non-expanding centers of origin. In South America, it is believed that people started growing potatoes, quinoa, and lima beans around the northern Andes Mountains (now in the country of Peru). They are also thought to have domesticated animals like guinea pigs and llamas. The reason South America is considered a nonexpanding center is because while it is evident that there was some early agricultural development, it stayed mostly in the same area. Instead, maize growers from Central America moved downward. In North America, people also grew grains along lakes and rivers until they, too, received knowledge of maize growing from the spread of Mesoamerican Neolithic peoples from the south.

The reason knowledge spread from Central America, overtaking the independent agricultural advances of North and South America, is likely because maize was a valuable crop. Maize was easy to grow throughout the Americas. It also grew quickly. In fact, more than one maize crop could grow and be harvested in a single growing season. The food provided was rich in calories to sustain villages and civilizations. The kernels were easy to store and could be made into a variety of dishes. Maize was certainly a miracle crop that took the Americas by storm.

CHAPTER 2
CHANGE FROM THE GROUND UP

Archaeologists have been studying clues for many years to learn how people—after so many years living as hunters and gatherers—were able to begin farming grains, vegetables, and fruits for food. They have uncovered a wealth of evidence that has helped them pinpoint where the changes happened and at what times. They found artifacts of the tools humans used both to store grain and to harvest it. Sometimes they found ancient grain! The story of Neolithic man's early farming can also be found in art. For example at Wadi Tashwinet, in what is now Libya, cave paintings dating from between 5000 and 2000 BCE show men hunting with dogs and herding goats and cattle.

TOOLS OF THE TRADE

Part of the process of learning how to farm was learning how to make tools for farming. While previously, people's tools were made for hunting, now they made new tools for farming, such as sickles for harvesting grain. Sickles were made of carved soft stone attached to a piece of wood. The tool was held in the hand and swung to chop down grain. Another tool used by Neolithic farmers was a grinding stone.

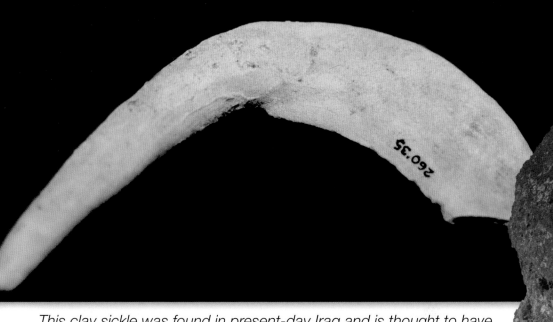

This clay sickle was found in present-day Iraq and is thought to have been made by the Sumerian people, one of the cultures of Mesopotamia. It dates to around 5000 to 4000 BCE.

This was made by carving out a hollow place in a large stone. A smaller stone could then be ground against it to pound grain into flour. Both sickles and grinding stones have been found in Neolithic settlements in the Near East and Asia.

Neolithic people, and even some Paleolithic people, used grain silos to store grain. Even before the agricultural revolution, people were beginning to eat wild grains—harvesting and storing them for later use. Storing grain is not considered to be agriculture, but it was a step in that direction. The earliest grain silos have been found in the Near East. A stone building dating to 11,400 years ago was found near the city of Jericho. It still had evidence of prehistoric grain inside. More grain silos have been found in the Fertile Crescent in what are now Syria, Jordan, Israel, and Turkey.

Happier but Not Healthier

It seems logical that having more reliable food sources would be a good thing for human health. However, research shows that the opposite is true. Humans actually became less healthy after the Neolithic Revolution. This cultural change led to changes in the human body. Because people weren't on the move all the time, they didn't need bones as dense or muscles as strong. So they lost these features gradually over time. Skeletons uncovered from this time also show a decrease in height. Neolithic people also had smaller skulls than their Paleolithic ancestors.

People ate much less meat as they came to rely more on grains. In some cases, this led to an iron deficiency because iron is found in meats. People were, in general, eating a much less varied diet than they did when they were hunters and gatherers, which made it harder to get all the nutrients they needed.

Dental health also suffered. As people settled down, they began grinding grain and cooking more foods. This led to softer foods and a more grain-based diet. While human skulls got smaller, it took longer for teeth to also adjust in size. This led to crowding of the teeth. Crowding is a problem because it leads to tight spaces between teeth where it's easy for bacteria to grow. Neolithic

people didn't have dental floss, and there is evidence that some suffered from periodontal disease, a disorder that attacks the gums and can lead to bone loss.

CHANGING NATURE

Neolithic people around the world were able to use their intelligence and new tools to harness the power of plants. In doing so, they domesticated wild species of plants. Domesticating doesn't just mean using wild species and controlling where they grow. It also means actually changing the species themselves to new ones that suit people's needs better. At first, Neolithic peoples farmed the same plants that grew wild. They took the seeds they found and planted them.

However, as time went on they learned how to choose the best seeds from the plants whose characteristics they liked the most. They would choose the grains that were the hardiest, easiest to grind, and tasted the best. This is a method that today we call selective breeding. By doing this over a period of time and several generations of the plants, people actually created new domestic species of grains and other plants.

A new species actually has different genetic information from its ancestors. This genetic information is held in the plant's DNA. Scientists discovered some of the first domesticated emmer wheat in Tell Aswad, in what is now Syria. By studying the DNA of the ancient grains, the scientists could see its past. They could see that the grain was significantly different from the wild grains growing in the same area. Neolithic farmers had left their mark.

The process of selective breeding of grains was similar in other

Emmer wheat, seen here, was one of the first domesticated species of wheat. Its scientific name is Triticum dicoccom.

parts of the world and for vegetables like legumes (such as beans) and roots like potatoes and taro as well. Gradually these plants also shifted as people continued to have an influence. For example, chickpeas are now one of the most common legumes grown in the world. These pale, round legumes are eaten in cuisines from the Middle East to Africa and India. The domestic version is fairly different from the

Chickpeas, shown growing here, are known by many names, including grams, garbanzo beans, Egyptian peas, and chana.

wild version of the chickpea, which now grows only in parts of Turkey.

The chickpea is thought to have first been domesticated around 9000 BCE in Turkey. Chickpeas are popular today because they pack a nutritional punch and are easy to store. They likely were popular in Neolithic times for the same reasons. The problem with wild chickpeas is that they ripen in winter, when they are also more susceptible to diseases. If the chickpeas caught a disease, it could wipe out the whole crop. In order to prevent this, Neolithic farmers chose the plants that produced chickpeas later in the season. Gradually, they changed the plants into a new species altogether. Today, these modern domesticated chickpeas are eaten all over the world. They produce legumes in the spring and summer months.

Thanks to agriculture, people were finding new ways to bend their environment and natural resources to suit their needs. The process happened over a relatively short time in different parts of the world. Not all attempts were successful, of course. Some plants ended up not working out. Sometimes this was because of the environment. Crops that were not able to thrive in one place could often be domesticated later in another part of the world. The grain rye was one of these agricultural duds in the Near East. It grew as a weed among the planted barley and wheat in areas of what are now Turkey and Iran, but the farmers of the Near East couldn't domesticate it. Instead rye seeds traveled to Europe, where the different climate and soil types helped to finally tame rye. A domestic strain of the grain was created in Europe around 3000 BCE.

CHAPTER 3
TAMING THE WILD BEASTS

Long before humans domesticated animals, they still relied on them for food. Ancient hunters roamed the forests and plains. They didn't just hunt small game to eat, they also needed large animals to help feed their families or clans. They didn't have large, settled communities yet, but they did hunt and travel in groups to which they were loyal. Humans are comparatively small and weak, so how did they bring down big game like bison and even bigger animals like mastodons and mammoths? After all, mammoths could be up to 13 feet (4 meters) high and weigh up to 12 tons (10,866 kilograms). The secret is that they used tools like flaked stone spear points and nets to enable them to attack the animals from a greater distance.

The other important secret is that they didn't do it alone. Humans hunted in packs. There was another animal species that also did this. In fact, it was one of only a few other species that was capable of bringing down a mammoth: wolves. Although they were competing for the same prey, these early hunters—humans and wolves—realized they could work together. Previously, they had hunted the game with mixed results. However, together they could both use their strengths to balance the other species' weaknesses. Wolves would track the prey, sometimes weaken it, and cut off its escape. Then human hunters with spears would

Much like wolves, humans hunted large game like mammoths in groups. Hunting could be extremely dangerous for people because large prey could and did fight back.

come in and finish the animal off. They would then share part of the kill with the wolves. This was beneficial to both humans and wolves. Humans didn't have to do all the work of tracking the animal, and wolves were spared having to get very close to the prey, which was often the most dangerous part of the hunt as a cornered prey animal can fight back.

This early hunting alliance may have paved the way for the domestication of the dog. As people and wolves got closer, humans may have started to raise wolf puppies themselves. Because they already live in packs, wolf puppies would have already had a natural instinct to do what they were told and join the

Man's Best Friend

These days, there are many breeds of dogs living among people. Some still help people by herding sheep, retrieving hunted game, or even aiding people with disabilities. Other dogs' main job is to look cute and provide companionship. Either way, many of these animals no longer resemble the wolves that were first domesticated by people.

For a long time, researchers believed that dogs were domesticated by Neolithic people along with other animals or shortly before. They originally pinpointed the time that dogs began to be domesticated between 16,000 and 11,000 BCE. However, in 2015, scientists found a bone from an ancient wolf in Siberia that dates to 35,000 years ago. By examining the DNA of the bone, they discovered it had some similarities to wolves and some to dogs. The scientists believe there might have been a three-way split in the evolution of the dog, the wolf, and the animal that left this bone. This suggests that the animal that this bone belonged to was domesticated by man almost twenty thousand years before the Neolithic Revolution.

"pack" they were born into. For this reason, dogs are one of the few animals that may have been domesticated prior to the Neolithic Revolution, when people were still living in small groups of nomadic hunters and gatherers.

Scientists believe that domestic sheep are descended from at least two different species of wild sheep. One is the mouflon, seen here, which lives in the Middle East.

CARNIVAL OF ANIMALS

Wolves and later their domesticated counterpart, dogs, were useful in the hunt. As humans settled down, though, they found many more useful animals. Herbivores (or plant eaters) such as goats, sheep, and cows could provide meat. Larger animals like oxen could also be used to help pull heavy things and plow fields. As with plant agriculture, the Near East saw the earliest domestication of flock animals. Sheep and goats were domesticated by 8000 BCE. Cows were domesticated around 7000 BCE. Pigs were likely first domesticated in China around 7000 BCE. Llamas and alpacas were first domesticated in South America around 4500 BCE. Horses were one of the later animals to be domesticated, which happened around 3600 BCE.

Scientists believe sheep were actually the very first domesticated herbivore. Today, sheep are raised for their wool and sometimes for their meat and milk. When people first domesticated them, sheep were mainly wanted for their meat. At an archaeological site called Shandir in what is now Iraq, researchers found the bones of many young sheep. They believe that Paleolithic people lived in the caves of Shandir. They didn't domesticate the sheep, but they did live with them. Much as occurred with the domestication of grains, there was a period before domestication of animals in which people were just doing their best to control wild species.

People began to be herders. They herded wild species of sheep and goats with them as they traveled in search of grass to feed their flocks. There were distinct advantages to herding a flock over hunting. A hunter's success largely depends on luck. If the hunter doesn't find good game that day or it manages to escape, then people go hungry. Alternatively, if the hunter has an excellent day and kills many animals, the meat will go bad if it is not eaten soon. Traveling with wild animals lets people kill an animal exactly when they needed meat.

CREATING NEW ANIMALS

The domestication of animals happened in much the way that domestication of plants did. People began choosing animals based on preferred traits. Over time, selective breeding had the same effect on animals as it

Several boar species still run wild in different parts of the world today. For example, this wild boar lives in the Forest of Rambouillet, in France.

did on plants. The traits people were mainly looking for in animals were being calmer and easier to control. By encouraging only animals that shared these characteristics to breed, over time people again created all new species. Wild boar became domestic pigs, and wild sheep, goats, and cows became closer to the domestic species we know today.

The domestication of animals, like that of plants, requires a lot of cooperation and organization among the people doing it. For example, if you have a few perfect sheep that are showing the characteristics you want, you can't eat them right away. You have to set those sheep

House cats today are used not only for their ability to kill vermin like mice, but also for companionship.

aside to encourage them to breed for the next generation. People were used to working together to stay alive, but this took a new level of co-operation for the good of the future. You might have to wait now, but in the end, you were rewarded with a better, stronger, easier to manage next generation of sheep.

As with the cooperative hunting of early man and wolves, domestication can have advantages for both humans and animals. The benefits for humankind are obvious. People can get food, labor, wool, skins, and bones for making tools from animals. However, animals can benefit, too. Those that are not killed for their meat but are kept for labor or to breed for the next generation generally have longer lives than their wild counterparts. They have food provided to them, as well as protection from predators.

An example of this mutually beneficial relationship is seen in the domestication of the cat. Cats were among the earliest animals to be domesticated. Archaeologists have found evidence of a cat burial in a Neolithic site Shillourokambos on the island of Cyprus around

8500 BCE. Researchers believe that wild cats likely were drawn to Neolithic settlements because of rats. People allowed them to hang around because they killed the rats that would otherwise eat their stored grain. Much like with the domestication of dogs, it was a natural and cooperative arrangement.

CAN ALL ANIMALS BE DOMESTICATED?

Since humans have been domesticating animals for so many thousands of years now, you might wonder why we haven't been able to domesticate them all. Why are there still so many species that are almost exclusively wild, such as giraffes, bears, and pandas?

There are a lot of reasons actually. Animals have to meet several criteria in order to be domesticated. Most were pretty gentle to start with and not prone to panic. While wolves aren't particularly gentle, their existing pack instincts made them more willing to take orders. Not all animals are so open to the idea of domestication. Few humans would want to tackle trying to raise wild bears.

Secondly, they have to be easy to care for. They can't require too much food or too specific a type of food. Otherwise they become more of a burden than a help. Also, they have to grow up quickly. Animals that take a long time to mature to an age at which they can be useful are naturally less appealing candidates for domestication.

CHAPTER 4
WHAT LED TO THE NEOLITHIC REVOLUTION?

For a long time, people have wondered why the Neolithic Revolution happened when it did. Why, after living a nomadic existence for a couple million years, did humans suddenly realize they could grow their own food? And how did people who were not in communication with each other arrive at the same idea at roughly the same time on different sides of the world?

Humans developed new tools to process their agricultural products. This tool is called a quern, and it was used for grinding corn into flour.

While agriculture and the domestication of animals could eventually result in an easier, more reliable way to supply food, at the outset it was actually more work. Suddenly people couldn't just spear an animal or snag some berries from the forest for an instant meal. They had to put some time and energy into sowing the seeds and then wait weeks or months for the grains and vegetables to mature. People had to create new tools and completely reinvent their social structure and way of life. They must have had some big reasons to change things up.

WAS THE WORLD WETTER OR DRIER?

There are a number of theories that scientists have suggested to answer these questions. One theory is that the climate changed. Suddenly it became drier, particularly in the Near East. Plants and animals that had once been abundant and easy to hunt and gather were suddenly harder to find. People had no choice but to change the ways they had done things. They had to adapt in order to survive. They learned to gather and store grain in the seasons when it grew well and gradually learned to plant seeds to grow it themselves. This lack of resources also forced humans into a closer relationship with animals. This theory was popular in the early 1900s.

However, scientists now believe that the climate at the time was actually getting wetter, not drier. Climate

THE POWER OF DISEASES

There were a lot of advantages to the Neolithic way of life. Neolithic people developed complex cultures and lived together in cities. However, there were some downsides to this new way of life. People living close together with each other and with animals led to the spread of disease. Strains of infectious diseases such as smallpox, measles, and tuberculosis have been found in the remains of Neolithic people.

While disease sounds like it would be a negative consequence, it actually didn't have a huge effect on population growth. While not everyone survived, many people who were exposed to diseases developed immunity. This resistance to disease was passed down genetically to their descendants. People in the Near East center and areas they initially spread to in Africa and Europe grew to have this immunity. It's possible this gave them a huge leg up much later.

In his book *Guns, Germs, and Steel: The Fates of Human Societies*, author Jared Diamond argues that the reason the Native Americans were nearly wiped out when European explorers arrived is because they had not developed an early culture of domesticating animals and living alongside them. This shows how the Neolithic Revolution continued to change the world thousands of years after it happened.

change may still have played a part by making the world an easier place to grow crops. If it was both wetter and warmer following the last Ice Age, it would have made stocking up on grain easier to do. Access to water certainly had an effect on Neolithic farmers. Certain areas of the world had advantages over others when the Neolithic Revolution began precisely because they had better access to water. It's not surprising that people living by rivers were the first to develop agriculture. Rivers provide everything from freshwater for drinking and for crops as well as transportation. Sources of water were important for farmers and also were an incentive for people to form a permanent settlement there. In the end, even if it was wetter instead

The remains of Neolithic dwellings built along the edges of lakes have been found in the Alps. This reconstruction of a Neolithic home overlooks Lake Ledro, in northern Italy.

of drier, climate change was likely a factor in people turning to agriculture. However, it may have just been one of many factors resulting in the Neolithic Revolution.

PEOPLE, PEOPLE EVERYWHERE

Another theory is that people had to change to a system of agriculture because populations were growing. While we know for sure that the population of the world increased a great deal after the Neolithic Revolution, there's a good chance it was increasing before that.

There is also proof that people were already starting to settle down and move around a little less even before discovering they could grow their own food. After all, before people domesticated species they were already herding wild animals and storing wild grains for later use.

Once people started stockpiling grain, they had more of a reason to stay in one place. Before they began actually planting the grain, they had already begun creating the buildings and tools—like grain silos and grinding stones—that would become useful when agriculture began in earnest. In fact, some archaeologists believe it was this population increase that led to the Neolithic Revolution instead of the other way around. According to this theory, as populations grew larger, they could no longer rely on hunting and gathering alone. They turned to agriculture as the only way to support their growing numbers.

CHAPTER 5
HUMANITY AFTER THE NEOLITHIC REVOLUTION

There are few aspects of modern, organized human civilization that don't have their roots in Neolithic invention. As people settled down, the world saw a surge in population. There were several reasons for this. First of all, food production was more efficient and more stable, so it could support a larger population. Secondly, women were able to have and care for more children because they didn't have to travel with them. Small settlements turned to towns, which in turn became

Skara Brae is a Neolithic village of stone houses located in Scotland. The site was occupied by people between 3200 and 2200 BCE.

cities. Some of these cities would form the foundations of the great civilizations of the Bronze Age.

From government to economy and trade to art and architecture, this time period was the start of some amazing advances in how humans lived. For the first time, they weren't just surviving. They were thriving. Some of the inventions of this time helped them manage their new systems and organize settlements better. Others were just for fun and because they had the time to devote to them.

BUILDING A HIERARCHY

Hierarchy and government came out of the necessity of having more rules and leadership with more people living together. In small groups of hunters and gatherers, everyone had roughly the same jobs. Work was often divided by gender, with men doing most of the hunting and women preparing the meat to eat, as well as gathering plants and berries. With more people settled in large groups and with some people farming the land or raising animals, more jobs were available. Someone had to build the houses that people lived in. Artists created pottery that wasn't just useful for storage but also had decorative qualities. Some people became priests and began conducting religious rituals. Now people could specialize in what they were most talented at. People could become experts at making the finest tools because they could devote all of their time to it.

When everyone was working together to find and prepare food, there was no sense of ownership. Now suddenly, there arose the idea of personal property. People felt like they owned the land they farmed or the food they grew from it. With this idea of personal property came many others. First of all, there arose a need for an economy. Goods were bartered, or traded, between

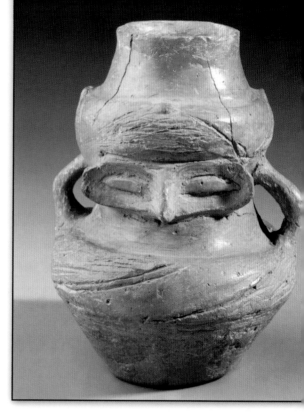

Some items from the Neolithic Revolution are both functional and decorative. This vase comes from a Neolithic settlement in what is now Bulgaria.

people for other goods or services they needed. If a farmer grew grain, for example, he could trade it for some pots to store it in or animal skins to make clothes from. With property ownership and economy came the idea of hierarchy. When everything wasn't shared and everything wasn't geared toward survival, then some people could possibly have more and others could possibly have less. Hierarchies weren't just about who had more land or food, but ultimately about who had more power.

Those who had more power gradually began to lead others. As governments formed, "government leader" also became a job some people could specialize in. Governments can provide many things for groups of people. They can provide protection. People living in settled groups are easier targets for other people to attack. They also have more to lose— buildings and farmland that can be destroyed and tools and animals that can be stolen. Soldiers and armies formed both to protect their cities and sometimes to attack other people's. Government and leadership can also provide stability and organization. Rules are necessary if large numbers of people live together. Some people rose to specialize in governing. These leaders helped manage disagreements between people, maintain law and order, punish rule breakers, control the army, and build structures like protective walls for the good of the people. Government leaders sometimes told stories and myths about how they had been anointed leaders by the gods. This helped make their position stronger and kept people from trying to overthrow them.

Hierarchy is not just about who has the most wealth and power. Hierarchy in society can also apply to characteristics of who a person is. For example, people can be lower or higher in the hierarchy based on their age or gender. Gender dynamics were changing during the Neolithic Revolution. As mentioned earlier, when people were hunters and gatherers, men tended to hunt and women tended to gather.

Men and women often had different jobs and responsibilities in Neolithic villages. Here women watch children, weave cloth, and grind grain into flour, while men mend a roof and herd animals.

Their roles had been different, but by and large men and women were held as equals.

During and after the Neolithic Revolution, attitudes about men and women began to change. Men did more of the farming and caring for animals. Women stayed in the home and prepared and cooked the food and made clothing. Men started to feel their work was more important to survival and that they were the ones who owned the land and food. Men began rising more in leadership, and women began taking a more subservient role. One exception to this was in the early settlement of Çatalhöyük, in what is now Turkey. Here men and women seemed to live very similar lives. Archaeologists studying remains in the Neolithic settlement determined that men and women ate the same foods, lived in the same way, did the same work, and ultimately were at the same level in the hierarchy. This was very different from many other Neolithic settlements in the Near East and around the world.

ARCHITECTURE AND ART

It's hard to imagine a time before people lived in houses and spent much of their time inside. Paleolithic hunters and gatherers lived in simple housing structures that could be erected quickly. They also lived in caves, when available. Neolithic housing became more advanced. People used mud to make bricks to create more permanent structures. Some of this early architecture has been uncovered in what are now Syria, Turkey, and parts of Europe. Later Neolithic housing has also been discovered in China.

The Çatalhöyük site is one of the most well preserved Neolithic cities yet discovered. The site was first discovered in 1950 and excavated in the 1960s. In 2012, it was declared a World Heritage Site. Archaeologists found an amazingly well-preserved city that had been lived in from 7400 BCE to 5500 BCE. It is full of many family dwellings, where thousands of people are thought to have permanently settled. The homes were made of mud brick and had no doors or paths between them. Instead people used wooden ladders

Çatalhöyük, in what is now Turkey, is the largest Neolithic site yet found. People living there walked on the roofs of buildings to get from place to place in the city.

to climb out of holes in the roofs. They would travel across the roofs of other homes to get across the city. The individual homes had hearths for cooking and smaller rooms for storage. A great deal of art was also found in Çatalhöyük, including murals, jewelry, and carved figurines.

Another example is Jericho, which is one of the oldest continuously occupied cities in the world. People lived there in Mesolithic and Neolithic times, and people still live there today. Neolithic people built stone houses with domed roofs between 10,000 and 9000 BCE. The population ranged from seventy homes to several thousand. What Jericho is

OTHER LEGACIES OF THE NEOLITHIC

Researchers believe that the Neolithic Revolution saw a rise in organized religion. Paleolithic people had spiritual beliefs, as suggested in their paintings and art. However, Neolithic people had many more complex rituals and religious practices. They had more time to devote to it. Thanks to job specialization, some members of society could devote themselves to becoming priests or other religious leaders. Evidence of belief in higher powers is seen in both Neolithic arts and in the construction of elaborate burial mounds, which suggest a belief in the afterlife.

Neolithic people also created the first calendars. They needed to be able to plan when to plant and harvest different crops. Most of these early calendars required tracking the phases of the moon. While researchers knew that Neolithic people had systems of timekeeping and date tracking, most written, recorded calendars they had found were from the Bronze Age. That changed in 2013, when scientists discovered a series of pits in Scotland that seemed to align with the phases of the moon. The site dates to 8000 BCE and is now known as one of the first calendars.

perhaps best known for is a huge stone wall surrounding the city. The 12-foot (3.6 m) high wall was made of stone. There was also a stone tower with a staircase inside containing stone steps. Archaeologists have questioned if the wall was to protect the city from human attackers, animal predators, or even floodwaters. Either way, moving the stones necessary to create the wall would have been a huge undertaking. It was the first known wall of its kind in the world.

In China, Neolithic structures have been discovered at the Banpo archaeological site along the Yellow River. Archaeologists found the remains of thatched roof houses supported by wood frames. They believe the town was lived in between 5000 and 4000 BCE. The settlement was surrounded by a moat. Archaeologists also found kilns for making pottery and graves showing that the dead had been buried with some ritual. The pottery produced here was truly unique among ancient civilizations. It was often dyed red and then carefully painted with symbols, drawings of animals, and even human faces.

THE DAWN OF CIVILIZATIONS

The Neolithic Revolution led to many advances that would pave the way for even more advances when the Bronze Age began around 3000 BCE. These included far-reaching trade networks, the use of metal tools, and new achievements in art and architecture. Like the Neolithic Revolution had, the major civiliza-

This cylinder seal with writing on it comes from the Sumerian civilization, which was the first civilization to form in Mesopotamia. This early example of writing dates to the 3rd century BCE.

tions of the Bronze Age sprung up along rivers. We call these civilizations the River Valley civilizations. Ancient Mesopotamia developed along the Tigris and Euphrates rivers in the Fertile Crescent. The peoples of Mesopotamia included the Sumerians, Assyrians, and Babylonians. They had complex cultures and religions. They even developed the first system of writing, called cuneiform. Along the Nile River, in Africa, the ancient Egyptian civilization sprung up. This civilization would last for thousands of years and leave behind a wealth of art, artifacts, language, and incredible feats of architecture that still stand today—the Great Pyramids. In China, the Yellow River, or Huang He, Civilization would form the foundation of many Chinese empires to come. From the Xia to the Shang dynasty, the Yellow River would remain an important center of economy, culture, and technology. The Indus Valley civilization extended along the Indus River in what is today India and Pakistan. It produced early boats and had a defined hierarchy called a caste system. At its height, this civilization had a population of several million people.

The groundwork not only for some of the greatest ancient civilizations on Earth but also for all of our current civilizations was laid in the Neolithic period. The Neolithic Revolution was one of the most impactful periods in human history. Every time you go to the grocery store, hang out in your house, pet your cat or dog, use government resources like roads or the post office, or even just eat an apple, you're taking advantage of aspects of civilization that were first started off by Neolithic people thousands of years before.

TIMELINE

c. 200,000 BCE *Homo sapiens* evolve in Africa.

c. 100,000 BCE Migrating humans reach the Near East and the Fertile Crescent.

c. 70,000 BCE Humans reach East Asia and China.

c. 33,000 BCE Scientists believe dogs were first domesticated from wolves.

c. 25,000–15,000 BCE Humans cross the Bering Strait (then a land bridge called Beringia) to reach the Americas.

c. 10,000 BCE The Neolithic Revolution begins in the Near East and China.

c. 9000 BCE The chickpea is first domesticated in Turkey. Emmer wheat is domesticated in the Fertile Crescent.

c. 8500 BCE The first cats are domesticated on the island of Cyprus.

c. 8000 BCE Sheep and goats are domesticated in the Fertile Crescent. A stone wall is built around the city of Jericho.

c. 7400–5500 BCE Neolithic people live in the city of Çatalhöyük in Turkey.

c. 7000 BCE The Neolithic Revolution begins in southern Mexico. In New Guinea, people begin farming taro in enclosed gardens. Pigs are first domesticated in China.

c. 5000–4000 BCE Neolithic people live at the Banpo site, along the Yellow River in China.

c. 4500 BCE Llamas and alpacas are domesticated in South America.

c. 3300 BCE A Bronze Age civilization begins in the Indus River Valley.

c. 3100 BCE Egypt is unified, creating one of the great River Valley Civilizations.

c. 3000–2000 BCE Rice growing spreads to Southeast Asia and the Indian Subcontinent.

GLOSSARY

archaeologists Scientists who study clues from the past to learn about human history.

barter To trade goods or services without money.

centers of origin Places around the world where agriculture independently began.

colonize To settle among, take over, or convert an area or a group of people.

deficiency A lack of something necessary.

divert To change the course of something.

DNA Deoxyribonucleic acid, a substance that carries the genetic code for living things.

domestication The process of changing wild plants and animals for human use.

economy The system by which goods, services, and wealth are held and exchanged.

herbivores Plant-eating animals.

hierarchy A system of organization in which some people are ranked higher and other people are ranked lower.

Ice Age A time during which ice sheets covered much of Asia, Europe, and North America that lasted from roughly 110,000 to 12,000 years ago.

immunity Protection from an illness, usually acquired by being exposed to the illness.

irrigation Moving water to places it otherwise wouldn't naturally flow in order to provide water for crops.

kiln An oven used to make pottery.

nomadic Traveling and moving around a lot as a way of life.

selective breeding Choosing to breed only animals or plants with characteristics favorable for the next generation.

species Living things grouped together because they share similar characteristics.

subservient Less important, expected to obey others.

supplement Something that completes or enhances something else but which cannot stand on its own.

FOR MORE INFORMATION

Archaeological Institute of America
656 Beacon Street, 6th Floor
Boston, MA 02215
(617) 353-9361
Website: https://www.archaeological.org
Since 1879, the Archaeological Institute of America (AIA) has
   promoted archaeological inquiry and public understanding of
   human history. Its research and events aim to foster an appreci-
   ation of diverse cultures and our shared humanity.

Canadian Archaeological Association
Department of Archaeology
Memorial University
St. John's NL A2C 5S7
Canada
Website: http://canadianarchaeology.com
Founded in 1968, this Canadian organization works to promote the
   field of archaeology and increase understanding about archaeo-
   logical research. Professional archaeologists, as well as students
   and members of the general public, are a welcome part of the
   organization.

The Field Museum
1400 S Lake Shore Drive
Chicago, IL 60605
(312) 922-9410
Website: https://www.fieldmuseum.org
Founded in 1893 as part of the World's Columbian Exposition, this

museum includes exhibits on both the science and history of the world. In 2015, the museum announced an exhibition on the Greek civilization beginning with its Neolithic origins.

Metropolitan Museum of Art
1000 5th Avenue
New York, NY 10028
(800) 662-3397
Website: http://www.metmuseum.org
This museum contains arts from the Neolithic period, especially in China, including pottery and carved jade jewelry. Its website also includes helpful background and timelines from this period.

National Museum of Denmark
Ny Vestergade 10
1471 København
Denmark
+45 33 13 44 11
Website: http://en.natmus.dk
This museum covers the Neolithic period as it occurred in Denmark and mainland Europe. The museum has artifacts including pottery and flint tools as well as information about the specifics of Neolithic cultures in Europe.

National Museum of Natural History
PO Box 37012 Smithsonian Institution
Washington, DC 20013
(202) 633-1000
Website: http://www.mnh.si.edu
Part of the Smithsonian Institution, the National Museum of Natural History provides artifacts and art from the Neolithic Age as well as information about that period.

Pointe-à-Callière
350 Place Royale
Montréal QC H2Y 3Y5
Canada
(514) 872-9150
Website: http://www.pacmusee.qc.ca/en/home
Pointe-à-Callière Museum serves as the museum of archaeology
    and history for the city of Montreal. While the museum generally
    focuses on the later history of the city, it does have exhibitions
    on early history, including the Neolithic period.

WEBSITES

Because of the changing nature of Internet links, Rosen
Publishing has developed an online list of websites related
to the subject of this book. This site is updated regularly.
Please use this link to access the list:

http://www.rosenlinks.com/FHEC/neo

FOR FURTHER READING

Brandon, S. G. F. *Beliefs, Rituals, and Symbols of Ancient Egypt, Mesopotamia, and the Fertile Crescent*. (Man, Myth & Magic). New York, NY: Cavendish Square Publishing, 2014.

Bray, Francesca, Peter A. Coclanis, Edda L. Fields-Black, and Dagmar Schafer. *Rice: Global Networks and Human History*. New York, NY: Cambridge University Press, 2015.

Bulliet, Richard, Daniel Headrick, Steven Hirsch, and Lyman Johnson. *The Earth and Its Peoples: A Global History*. 6th ed. Stamford, CT: Cengage Learning, 2014.

Butler, Alan. *Sheep: The Remarkable Story of the Humble Animal That Built the Modern World*. London, UK: John Hunt Publishing, 2013.

Currier, Richard L. *Unbound: How Eight Technologies Made Us Human, Transformed Society, and Brought Our World to the Brink*. New York, NY: Arcade Publishing, 2015.

Dorling Kindersley. *Early People* (Eye Wonder). New York, NY: DK Publishing, 2015.

Fullman, Joseph. *Ancient Civilizations* (DK Eyewitness Books). New York, NY: DK Publishing, 2013.

Hodder, Ian. *The Leopard's Tale: Revealing the Mysteries of Çatalhöyük*. London, UK: Thames and Hudson, 2011.

Pipe, Jim, and Zack McLaughlin. *How People Lived*. New York, NY: DK Publishing, 2011.

Romer, John. *A History of Ancient Egypt: From the First Farmers to the Great Pyramid*. New York, NY: St. Martin's Press, 2012.

Wang, Xiaoming, and Richard H. Tedford. *Dogs: Their Fossil Relatives and Evolutionary History*. New York, NY: Columbia University Press, 2010.

Zohard, Daniel, Maria Hopf, and Ehud Weiss. *Domestication of Plants in the Old World*. New York, NY: Oxford University Press, 2012.

BIBLIOGRAPHY

Anadolu Agency. "Çatalhöyük Excavations Reveal Gender
    Equality in Ancient Settled Life." *Hürriyet Daily News*.
    Retrieved January 9, 2016 (http://www.hurriyetdailynews
    .com/catalhoyuk-excavations-reveal-gender-equality
    -in-ancient-settled-lifeaspx?pageID=238&nID=72411
    &NewsCatID=375).

Diamond, Jared. *Guns, Germs, and Steel: The Fates of Human
    Societies*. New York, NY: W. W. Norton and Company, 1997.

Dunham, Will. "Dog Domestication Much Older than Previously
    Known." *Scientific American*, May 21, 2015 (http://www
    .scientificamerican.com/articledog-domestication-much
    -older-than-previously-known).

Global Rice Science Partnership. "History of Rice Cultivation."
    Ricepedia. Retrieved January 9, 2016 (http://ricepedia.org/
    culture/history-of-rice-cultivation).

Goodale, Nathan, Heather Otis, William Andrefsky, and
    Ian Kuijt. "Sickle Blade Life-history and the Transition to
    Agriculture: An Early Neolithic Case Study from Southwest
    Asia." *Journal of Archaeological Science*, September 14,
    2009 (http://libarts.wsu.edu/anthro/pdf/Goodale%20et%20
    al%20JAS.pdf).

Grimm, David. "Feature: Solving the Mystery of Dog
    Domestication." *Science*, April 16, 2015 (http://news
    .sciencemag.org/archaeology/2015/12feature-solving
    -mystery-dog-domestication).

Hansen, Casper Worm, Peter Sandholt Jensen, and Christian Skovsgaard. "Gender Roles and Agricultural History: The Neolithic Inheritance." University of Copenhagen, Department of Economics, 2012 (http://www.econ.ku.dk/mehr/calendar/seminars/30112012/Hansen_et_al___2012__pdf.pdf).

Latham, Katherine. "Human Health and the Neolithic Revolution: An Overview of Impacts of the Agricultural Transition on Oral Health, Epidemiology, and the Human Body." University of Nebraska, 2013 (http://digitalcommons.unl.edu/cgi/viewcontent.cgi?article=1186&context=nebanthro).

Mazoyer, Marcel, and Laurence Roudart. *A History of World Agriculture: From the Neolithic Age to the Current Crisis*. New York, NY: Monthly Review Press, 2006.

Mithem, Steven. *After the Ice Age: A Global Human History, 20,000–5000 BC*. Cambridge, MA: Harvard University Press, 2006.

Roach, John. "Was Papua New Guinea an Early Agriculture Pioneer?" *National Geographic*. June 23, 2003 (http://news.nationalgeographic.com/news/2003/06/0623_030623_kukagriculture.html).

Simmons, Alan H. *The Neolithic Revolution in the Near East: Transforming the Human Landscape*. Tucson, AZ: The University of Arizona Press, 2010.

INDEX

A

animals, domestication of, 7, 10, 11, 15, 19, 27–34, 36, 37,39
architecture, 8, 41, 45–46, 48, 49
art, 10, 20, 41, 45–46, 47, 48, 49
Assyrians, 49
avocados, 15

B

Babylonians, 49
Banpo site, 48
bartering, 42
beans, 16, 19, 24
Bronze Age, 8, 41, 47, 48, 49

C

calendars, 47
caste systems, 50
Çatalhöyük, 44–46
cats, 33–34, 50
cave paintings, 10, 20
centers of origin, 10–12, 14–17
chickpeas, 24–25
climate change, 36, 38
cuneiform, 49

D

Danube River, 17
Diamond, Jared, 37
diseases, 23, 25, 37
DNA, 24, 29
dogs, 20, 28, 29, 30, 34, 50

E

economies, 8, 41, 42, 50

Egyptians, 18, 49
emmer wheat, 12, 24
Euphrates River, 12, 49

F

Fertile Crescent, 8, 21, 49

G

gender roles, 41, 43–45
governments, 6, 8, 41, 43, 50
grain silos, 21, 39
Great Pyramids, 49
Guns, Germs, and Steel, 37

H

health, changes in, 22–23
herbivores, 30, 31
hierarchies, 8, 41–45, 50
History of World Agriculture, The, 11
Homo sapiens, 6
Huang He civilization, 49

I

Ice Age, 38
immunity, 37
Indus River, 50
Indus Valley civilization, 50
iron deficiency, 22
irrigation, 17

J

Jericho, 13, 21, 46
Jordan River Valley, 13

M

maize, 15, 16, 18, 19
Mesoamerica, 14, 15–16, 19
Mesolithic period, 8, 9, 10, 46
Mesopotamia, 49
Middle Stone Age, 9
Moyozer, Marcel, 11

N

Native Americans, 37
Natufian, 13
New Guinea, 11, 16–17, 18
New Stone Age, 8
Nile River, 12, 18, 49

O

Old Stone Age, 9

P

Paleolithic period, 8, 9, 10, 21,
    22, 31, 45, 47
plants, domestication of, 10, 11,
    14, 16–17, 20–26, 31, 32
property ownership, 42

Q

quinoa, 19

R

religion, 47, 49
rice, 14, 18
River Valley Civilizations, 49

S

selective breeding, 23–24, 31–32
Shandir, 31
Shang dynasty, 49
slash-and-burn farming, 17

squash, 15, 16
stone carvings, 10, 13, 20
Sumerians, 49

T

taro, 16, 18, 24
Tigris River, 12, 49
tools, 8, 9, 10, 17, 18, 20–21, 23,
    27, 33, 36, 39, 41, 43, 48

W

Wadi Tashwinet, 20
World Heritage Site, 45

X

Xia dynasty, 49

Y

Yangshao civilization, 12
Yangtze River, 14
Yellow River, 12, 48,
    49–50

ABOUT THE AUTHOR

Susan Meyer is the author of more than fifteen young adult titles. She is a fan of organized agriculture and attempts, with middling results, to grow her own vegetables. Meyer lives in Austin, Texas, with her husband, Sam, and her domestic cat, Dinah.

PHOTO CREDITS

Cover, p. 3 © iStockphoto.com/davidevison; p. 7 Jim Richardson/National Geographic Image Collection/Getty Images; p. 11 Dorling Kindersley/Getty Images; p. 14 O. Louis Mazzatenta/National Geographic Image Collection/Getty Images; p. 15 Ovu0ng/Shutterstock.com; p. 16 © iStock.com/Kalulu; p. 18 Pasquale Sorrentino/Science Source; p. 21 Universal History Archive/Universal Images Group/Getty Images; p. 24 © Nature Picture Library/Alamy Stock Photo; p. 25 Sever180/Shutterstock.com; p. 28 © dieKleinert/Alamy Stock Photo; p. 30 ullstein bild/Getty Images; p. 32 Joel Saget/AFP/Getty Images; p. 33 Milan Vachal/Shutterstock.com; p. 35 Print Collector/Hulton Archives/Getty Images; p. 38 francesco de marco/Shutterstock.com; p. 40 Patrick Dieudonne/robertharding/Getty Images; p. 42 Danita Delimont/Gallo Images/Getty Images; p. 44 Private Collection/ © Look and Learn/Bridgeman Images; p. 46 muratart/Shutterstock.com; p. 49 DEA/G. Dagli Orti/De Agostini/Getty Images; back cover, interior pages (rock formation) © iStockphoto.com/franck-reporter; interior pages (evolution illustration) © iStockphoto.com/Xrisca30, (rocky texture) © iStockphoto.com/velkol

Designer: Matt Cauli; Editor: Amelie von Zumbusch; Photo Researcher: Bruce Donnola